MAGNETISM AND ELECTRICITY
BOOK 6

ALSO BY
ROBERT FRIEDHOFFER

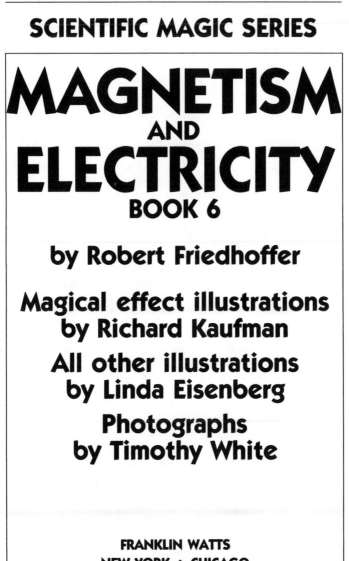

SCIENTIFIC MAGIC SERIES

MAGNETISM
AND
ELECTRICITY
BOOK 6

by Robert Friedhoffer

Magical effect illustrations
by Richard Kaufman

All other illustrations
by Linda Eisenberg

Photographs
by Timothy White

FRANKLIN WATTS
NEW YORK ◆ CHICAGO
LONDON ◆ TORONTO ◆ SYDNEY

Library of Congress Cataloging-in-Publication Data

Friedhoffer, Robert.
Magnetism and electricity / by Robert Friedhoffer ; magical effect
illustrations by Richard Kaufman ; other illustrations by Linda
Eisenberg ; photography by Timothy White.
p.   cm.—(Scientific magic series ; bk. 6)
Includes bibliographical references (p.   ) and index.
Summary: This sixth volume in a six-volume series of books using
magic tricks and activities to illustrate scientific principles
features experiments with magnetism and electricity.
ISBN 0-531-11084-2
1. Magnetism—Juvenile literature.   2. Magnetism—Experiments—
Juvenile literature.   3. Electricity—Juvenile literature.
4. Electricity—Experiments—Juvenile literature.   5. Scientific
recreations—Juvenile literature. [1. Magnetism—Experiments.
2. Electricity—Experiments.   3. Experiments.   4. Scientific
recreations.   5. Magic tricks.] I. Kaufman, Richard, ill.
II. Eisenberg, Linda, ill.   III. White, Timothy, ill.   IV. Title.
V. Series: Friedhoffer, Robert. Scientific magic series ; bk. 6.
QC753.7.F75   1992
537'.078—dc20   92-19223   CIP   AC

Printed in the United States of America
6 5 4 3 2 1

CONTENTS

To the memory of the Wolens:
Yetta, Albert, and Seymour
and to
the continued good health of
Robert "Big Bob" Wolen
for his help and encouragement
while writing this seemingly never-ending
series of books

ACKNOWLEDGMENTS

I would first like to thank Microsoft Corporation for providing MS Windows™ and MS Word for Windows™ and Logitech, Inc. for providing a Mouseman™ Cordless mouse and a Scanman® Model 256. These marvelous products lightened the physical chores of writing and were a joy to work with.

I would like to thank the following people for helping make this book possible by supplying ideas, encouragement, and/or inspiration: Sir Isaac Newton, Leibniz, Galileo, Otto van Guericke, John Blake, John Wilkins, Rene Descartes, David Brewster, Carl Stenquist, Iris Rosoff, Martin Gardner, Peter and Jackie Monticup, Martin Tamny, Renee Waldinger, Richard Wactler, Joanie Warner, Brian Werther, Gary Wilner, Art Kahn, Torkova and Meier Yedid, Tim White, Linda Eisenberg, Richard Kaufman, Howard MacNeil, Alicia Ho White, Constantine "Gus" Philippas, Russel Ward, and Laura Hughes.

"The whole of science is nothing more than a
refinement of everyday thinking."
—Albert Einstein, *Out of My Later Years*

"Science is the best magic."
—Bob Friedhoffer

INTRODUCTION

Even though this series of six books doesn't have to be read consecutively, it might help the beginning magical scientist to do so. The basics of physics start in the first book. Each succeeding book builds upon the knowledge of the one before. The tricks, experiments, and betchas are in there to help you have fun and get the most that you possibly can out of each book.

When you perform the experiments, you might want to *keep a notebook or diary of all of your results*. In keeping the diary, you will be following in the footsteps of such great scientists of the world as Madame Marie Sklodowska Curie (1867–1934)— radiation; Rosalind Elsie Franklin (1920–1958)— DNA; Galileo Galilei (1564–1642)—astronomy, mathematics, and physics; and Albert Einstein (1879–1955)—theoretical physics.

The tricks are laid out with EFFECT first, to let you have an idea of what the trick is about. Next comes the PROPS section, so you'll know what "stuff" you need. Then comes the METHOD, or ROU-TINE part, which fully explains the workings of the trick. The NOTES that are at the very end of the trick try to tie the scientific principle in with the routine.

If you want to teach the science behind the tricks, you might want to explain the workings of the experiments to your friends. If you want to be a magician, you're better off not telling your friends how the tricks work. If your friends know the secrets to the trick, there is no magic.

To become a magician, you need to know all of the secrets of magic. To learn many of the secrets, you have to know something about science. You'll learn many of the "secrets" of science in this series of books.

When you learn the science, you become the magician. You just have to learn how to present the scientific principle in a mystifying way.

If you have any science tricks of your own that you think you would like to share with others, please send them along to me in care of my publisher:

FRANKLIN WATTS
95 Madison Avenue
New York, New York 10016

Perhaps I'll have room to place your trick with your name next to it in my next science/magic book. Study hard and work hard, and the universe can be yours.

Bob Friedhoffer

AN OPEN LETTER TO ALL
WHO READ THIS BOOK

Greetings!

Physics—the study of matter and energy and how they affect each other—is all around us! Pretty scary thought, eh? Not really. Physics doesn't have to be frightening at all. There's little that we do every day that doesn't involve physics.

Here's a list of some things that use physics: riding skateboards and bicycles, playing video games, watching TV, listening to stereos, baking a cake, cooking an egg, drawing pictures, driving a car, working on your computer, shooting an arrow, playing the piano or guitar, turning on your shower, doing magic tricks, and playing practical jokes. In other words, physics is everywhere, and it can be fun if you look at it with an open mind.

I've written this series with as light a touch as possible. I've put in very little math, and all of the experiments can be done at or near your home for practically no expense. Almost all of the magic tricks are done with stuff you find around the house.

When you perform the magic, remember that if you want to fool your friends, you should keep the secret to yourself. If someone wants to know, "How did you do that trick?" you can honestly say, "I did it with science—physics, to be exact."

If you wish to share any secrets with your friends, don't tell them how the tricks are done; let them read the book. They can buy it or take it out of the library. If you tell them how you do a trick and they don't have to put any effort into finding out the secret, they won't respect you or the trick.

I hope that you enjoy the books in this series, and all of the experiments, tricks, and betchas that you'll find inside.

NOTE: About the use of the metric system and English system in this book: Although the metric system is easier to use, both systems are used in this series of books. In some experiments and tricks, only metric measurements are used; in others, only the English system. In still others, both are given.

Bob Friedhoffer
aka The Madman of Magic

NATURAL MAGNETS

Back in ancient Greece, about 600 B.C., the scientists/philosophers of the day knew about magnets, although they weren't the kind of magnets that we're used to today. The only magnets known then were rocks we call *magnetite*, or *lodestone*. Lodestones are composed of magnetic iron oxide (Fe_3O_4), which is a common iron ore.

Lodestones were the first magnets.

It is thought that the Chinese were the first to use these magnetic rocks as compasses to chart directions on the open sea. They would take a small fragment of lodestone and hang it by a string from an overhead ship beam. The rock would "magically" align itself in a north–south direction.

Even though the ancients knew that lodestone attracted iron, they didn't know why. There was nothing connecting the lodestone and the iron, so why was there an attraction?

Today we use artificial magnets, which are composed of steel alloys and certain ceramics combined with rare earth compounds.

MAGNETIC MATERIALS

Artificial magnets are classified as either *permanent* or *temporary*.

There are a number of materials that can be magnetized, or made temporarily magnetic. The element iron (Fe), for instance, has exceptional magnetic features. Steel, being an alloy of iron and other elements, has similar magnetic properties. The elements cobalt (Co) and nickel (Ni) are slightly magnetic. Alloys that are especially useful as temporary magnets are carbon steel (iron and carbon), permalloy (iron and nickel), alnico (*al*uminum, *ni*ckel, *co*balt, and iron), and tungsten steel (tungsten, iron, and carbon).

Experiment 1
APPARATUS

a piece of lodestone (Frey Scientific catalog, pg. 540—#2173 and #2174)

a small rock, about the same size as the lodestone

Enamel paint (used for models; available at hobby shops)

a toothpick

2 pieces of thread

PROCEDURE

Tie one piece of the thread around the lodestone. Mark a point on one edge of the lodestone with the paint and toothpick. (See illustration.) Tie the thread around the rock. Mark a point on one edge of the rock with the paint and toothpick.

PAINT

LODESTONE

Go outside to a clear area, away from power lines and buildings. Hold the end of the thread and let the lodestone swing freely. When it has stopped swinging, note the direction in which the painted spot on the lodestone is pointing.

Slowly turn around. Notice how the marked spot on the lodestone always points in the same direction.

Now hold the other end of the thread and let the rock swing freely. When it has stopped swinging, note the direction in which the painted spot on the rock is facing.

Again, slowly turn around. Notice how the marked spot on the rock seems to point in no direction in particular.

NOTE: The lodestone seems to always point in one particular direction, while the rock does not.

Now you can understand how the ancient Chinese might have used the lodestone to help navigate. Once they knew that the lodestone always pointed in the same direction, they could be at sea, out of sight of land, and still know which way they were headed.

This was the first compass. The sailors didn't know how or why the lodestone worked; they just knew that it did.

But the lodestone showed only the general direction of north and south. Sailors still needed to use the position of fixed stars to navigate properly.

In a later section we'll discuss why lodestones and other magnets always point in the same direction.

Betcha 1

"I betcha that I can use a screwdriver for two things. Not only can I use it to turn a screw, but I can also use it to pick up a screw that I drop on the floor.

"I will not attach anything sticky to the screwdriver, like glue, tape, or chewing gum."

PROPS
   a steel screwdriver (make sure that the screwdriver is not magnetized)
   a magnet
   a small iron or steel screw

METHOD
Drop the screw on the floor and let your friend try to pick it up. When he or she is unable to do so, take the magnet out of your pocket and stroke it along

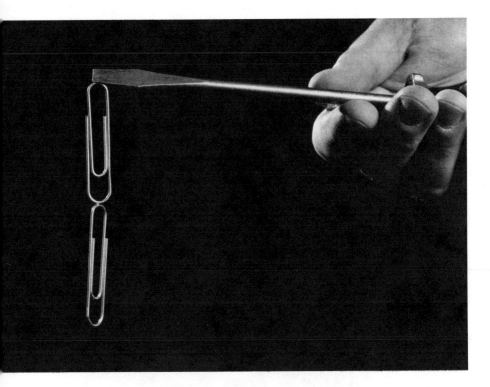

You can use a magnetized screwdriver to pick up nails, screws, paper clips, or any other small iron or steel objects.

the length of the screwdriver, from the handle to the tip. Just stroke it in one direction. After you stroke the blade a few times (ten strokes should do it), you will have magnetized the screwdriver. This means that you will have turned it into a temporary magnet.

At this point, you will be able to pick up a steel or iron screw with the tip of the screwdriver.

MAGNETIC POLES

As seen in Betcha 1, it is not very difficult to make a bar of iron or steel into a magnet. You can use the same method to magnetize almost any iron or steel bar.

When a bar of iron or steel is magnetized, the ends of the bar seem to have the greatest amount of attraction, while the middle portion has the least. The ends of the bar magnet are called the *magnetic poles*. If you plunge the ends of a bar magnet into iron filings, the filings cling to the ends of the bar like a heavy coating of whiskers.

If you hang a bar magnet from a thread as you did to the lodestone, the end that points toward the north is called the *north pole*, or simply *N*. The end that points south is the *south pole*, or *S*.

Experiment 2

APPARATUS

    a piece of thread
    2 bar magnets
    cellophane tape
    a thumbtack

PROCEDURE

PART 1

    Tie the thread around the middle of one magnet so that the magnet is balanced. To help secure the thread in place, tape it.

    Repeat the experiment that you did with the lodestone (Experiment 1).

MAGNETIC NORTH THATAWAY ⟶

NOTE: The magnet will act just like the lodestone; one end will generally point in the same direction all of the time.

You will find that the north pole of the magnet will point in a northerly direction and the south pole in a southerly direction. This is due to the earth's magnetic poles (see pages 39–40).

PART 2

Using the thumbtack, attach one end of the thread tied around the magnet to an overhead beam, such as the lintel of a door frame. Call this magnet #1. The second magnet is #2.

Once #1 has stopped swinging, bring #2 toward it. First, approach #1's north pole with the south pole of #2. Try to keep them apart. What happens?

Next, approach #1's south pole with the north pole of #2. What happens?

Once #1 has stopped swinging, approach its north pole with the north pole of #2. Try to make them touch while approaching very slowly. What happens?

Next, approach #1's south pole with the south pole of #2. What happens?

NOTE: The opposite poles (north and south) of the

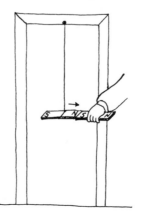

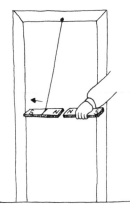

magnets attract each other. The same poles (north and north, south and south) repel each other.

We can sum this up by saying: Like poles (N/N and S/S) repel. Unlike poles (N/S and S/N) attract.

If a bar magnet is cut in half, each new end becomes a pole. The original uncut ends stay the same (north or south), while the new ends become the opposite poles. It doesn't matter how many times you slice up

a bar magnet—each time it is cut, new poles are established at the cut ends.

MAGNETIC THEORY

The individual molecules in an iron bar act as tiny magnets. These individual molecules of iron are clustered in areas called *domains*. In a nonmagnetized piece of iron, the molecules are in disarray, jumbled in a random pattern. When we magnetize an iron bar by stroking it with a magnet, as we did

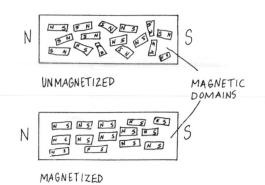

N · UNMAGNETIZED · S

MAGNETIC DOMAINS

N · MAGNETIZED · S

the screwdriver in Betcha 1, the molecules of iron line up, all of them facing the same direction. The north and south poles at the ends of the bar are determined by the strengths of the combined domains.

INDUCED MAGNETISM

If a magnet is touched to one end of an iron or steel straight pin, and the end of the pin is touched to another straight pin, the first pin will act as a magnet and pick up the second. This is an example of *induced magnetism*. The magnet keeps the iron mole-

cules of the straight pin aligned and turns the first pin into a temporary magnet.

**"CRDL®" is a toy that works by
induced magnetism. (Courtesy of CRDL®)**

Trick 1
The Balancing Coin
EFFECT: Two pennies are placed on the table. Pick one up and hold it with your fingertips. Next, balance the edge of the second penny on the top edge of the first one. Give the pennies to your friends. They won't be able to do this trick.

PROPS
   2 copper-coated 1943 U.S pennies (available from magicians' supply stores)
   a small permanent magnet

NOTE: This complete trick is available from magic stores under the name *E-Z Magic Penny Balancer.*

METHOD
Until 1989 all U.S. pennies were made of copper, a nonmagnetic metal, except for pennies minted in 1943, which were made from steel, a magnetic alloy. A number of 1943 pennies were coated with copper for the express purpose of performing this trick.
   Conceal the magnet at your fingertips. Place the first penny on top of the magnet. You can now easily balance the second penny on top of the first one.

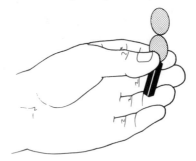

   This trick works because of magnetic induction. The first penny acts as a magnet and attracts the second steel penny.
   When your friends ask you about the trick the next day, you can drive them crazy by telling them that you did it with a magnet. Don't tell them about the copper-coated steel coins. They'll go home and try the trick and think that you lied to them, because pennies other than those struck in 1943 are not affected by magnets.

Trick 2
Linking Paper Clips

EFFECT: You display a handful of unlinked paper clips to your audience. You then drop them into a paper cup, say the magic word or make a magic gesture, then turn the cup upside down. The clips come out linked together.

PROPS
    2 dozen copper-coated steel paper clips
    a large paper cup (with a divider down the middle)
    a magnet
    glue

SETUP
Glue the magnet to one side of the divided cup, at the bottom. Link twelve of the clips together. Place the linked paper clips in the side of the paper cup without the magnet.

The setup. Note that the clips in the bottom of the cup are already linked together.

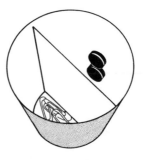

METHOD
When you drop the unlinked paper clips into the cup, make sure that they go in the side with the magnet. After you make a magical gesture, turn the cup upside down. The linked clips will fall out; the loose clips will cling to the magnet and to each other through induced magnetism and stay in the cup.

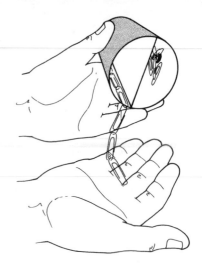

When you drop the linked clips into your open hand, don't "flash" the inside of the cup to your audience.

Casually crush the cup at the end of the trick and toss it into the garbage pail. Just remember to retrieve it after your performance so you won't lose the magnet.

MAGNETIC FIELDS

As you've seen, magnets have the ability to exert a force on other magnets or pieces of magnetic material some distance away. The reason that they can do this is because magnets are surrounded by a *magnetic field*. The field is strongest near a magnet. It becomes weaker farther away from a magnet. You can actually see magnetic fields with *Magnaview Paper/Film*, which is available from Edmund Scientific or Magnet Sales & Mfg. Co. 11248 Playa Court, Culver City, California 90230. If you place a magnet on Magnaview, you will see the magnetic lines of force. A messier way to see the lines of force follows.

Experiment 3
APPARATUS
    a thin piece of cardboard
    iron filings
    various magnets (horseshoe, bar, circular, square)

PROCEDURE

Place the cardboard on top of a magnet. Sprinkle a small amount of iron filings on top of the cardboard. Lightly tap the cardboard with your fingertip.

Iron filings illustrate magnetic fields of force.

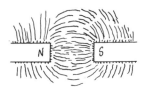

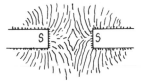

NOTE: You will see the iron filings start to line up, making straight lines and parts of circles. The filings arrange themselves along the lines of magnetic force.

For each magnet used, draw the lines of force as they appear on the cardboard.

Put two magnets under the cardboard and observe their combined lines of magnetic force. First put like pole to like pole. Next, unlike pole to unlike pole.

Try to put a piece of nonmagnetized iron bar between the unlike poles. What happens?

NOTE: You can use an empty plastic shoe box instead of a piece of cardboard. Place the shoe box over the magnet, then slowly sprinkle the iron filings into the box. This will allow you to see the magnetic lines of force without spilling iron filings and causing a mess.

WAYS TO MAGNETIZE

There are a number of ways to magnetize, or cause molecules of iron to line up in one direction.

1. Stroke a steel bar with a permanent magnet, as we did in Betcha 1. The magnet's poles attract the opposite poles of the domains. When the opposite poles are attracted, the molecules of iron in the steel line up in one direction, resulting in a temporary magnet.

2. Wrap a piece of insulated electrical wire around a piece of iron or steel. When a direct current (see page 59) is sent through the wire, steel becomes a permanent magnet and iron becomes a temporary magnet. When the electricity stops flowing, the iron loses its magnetism, while the steel usually stays magnetic.

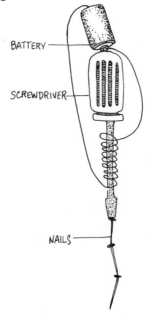

BATTERY

SCREWDRIVER

NAILS

3. Align a bar of steel in a north–south direction. (You can do Experiment 2 to determine north and

south.) Bring the end of the bar that points north to a downward angle of 75° to the horizontal. Rest that end firmly on the ground.

If you smash the bar with a hammer a few times, the bar should now be magnetized. The end of the bar that was pointing downward becomes the north

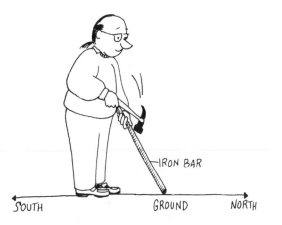

pole, the other end the south pole. The magnetic field generated by the earth lines up the domains in the bar when the molecules are jolted by the hammer striking the bar.

Experiment 4
APPARATUS
> an iron tenpenny nail
> 6 feet of 18-gauge insulated electrical wire
> a dry cell battery
> a collection of items made of copper, aluminum, iron, and steel (for example, paper clips, nails, and screws)

PROCEDURE
Spread the screws, nails, and so on on a table. Wrap the center of the wire around the iron tenpenny nail.

Connect the ends of the wire to the battery terminals, one end to each terminal. Touch the wire-wrapped nail to each item. Which items are affected? Which are not?

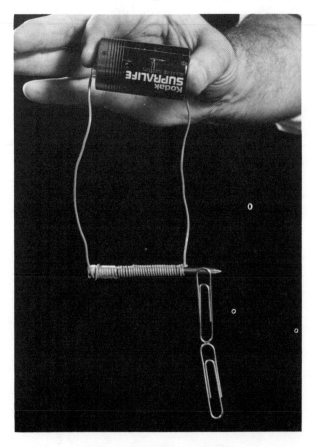

**An iron nail can be turned
into an electromagnet.**

NOTE: You have constructed an *electromagnet*. Electromagnets have many uses in everyday life. One place that you will find them is in scrap metal

yards, where they are used to move heavy pieces of iron, such as old cars. Electromagnets are used because once the scrap metal is moved and the electricity is turned off, the magnetic attraction ceases. In other words, they can pick up scrap metal junk cars from one place and drop it in another.

Trick 3
The Light and Heavy Chest
In 1856 Jean Eugene Robert-Houdin, a French magician often referred to as the "father of modern magic," went to Algeria to perform his wonders there. The following is excerpted from *The Memoirs of Robert-Houdin*, first published in the United States in 1859.

> *It is known that the majority of revolts which have to be suppressed in Algeria are excited by intriguers, who say they are inspired by the Prophet, and are regarded by the Arabs as envoys of God on earth to deliver them from the oppression of the Roumi (Christians).*
>
> *These false prophets and holy Marabouts, who are no more sorcerers than I am, and indeed even less so, still contrive to influence the fanaticism of their co-reli-*

gionists by tricks as primitive as are the spectators before whom they are performed.

The government was, therefore, anxious to destroy their pernicious influence, and reckoned on me to do so. They hoped, with reason, by the aid of my experiments, to prove to the Arabs that the tricks of the Marabouts were mere child's play, and owing to their simplicity could not be done by an envoy from Heaven, which also led us very naturally to show them that we are their superiors in everything, *and as for sorcerers, there are none like the French.*

I advanced with my box in my hand to the center of the "practible" communicating from the stage to the pit; then addressing the Arabs, I said to them:

"From what you have witnessed, you will attribute a supernatural power to me, and you are right. I will give you a new proof of my marvelous authority, by showing that I can deprive the most powerful man of his strength and restore it at my will. Anyone who thinks himself strong enough to try the experiment may draw near me."

(I spoke slowly, in order to give the interpreter time to translate my words.)

An Arab of middle height, but well built and muscular, like many of the Arabs are, came to my side with sufficient assurance.

"Are you very strong?" I said to him, measuring him from head to foot.

"Oh yes!" he replied carelessly.

"Are you sure you will always remain so?"

"Quite sure."

"You are mistaken, for in an instant I will rob you of your strength, and you shall become as a little child."

The Arab smiled disdainfully as a sign of his incredulity.

"Stay," I continued; "Lift up this box."

The Arab stooped, lifted up the box, and said to me coldly, "Is that all?"

"Wait———!" I replied.

Then, with all possible gravity, I made an imposing gesture and solemnly pronounced the words:

"Behold! you are weaker than a woman; now try to lift the box."

The Hercules, quite cool as to my conjuration, seized the box once again by the handle and gave it a violent tug, but this time the box resisted, and in spite of his most vigorous attacks would not budge an inch.

The Arab vainly expended on this box a strength that would have raised an enormous weight, until, at length, exhausted, panting, and red with anger, he stopped, became thoughtful, and began to comprehend the influences of magic.

METHOD

Robert-Houdin used a small chest constructed of wood. The bottom of the box was actually an iron plate covered by wood.

Underneath the runway was an extremely powerful electromagnet. Robert-Houdin signaled an assistant, and the electromagnet was turned on. The man from the audience had no chance of lifting the box because the force exerted by the electromagnet was greater than the man's own strength.

DEMAGNETIZING

There are a number of reasons why you might want to demagnetize something. A screwdriver with an insulated handle or a wind-up watch that is spring-powered might become accidentally magnetized.

Here are three ways to demagnetize a screwdriver with an insulated handle.

1. Making sure that the screwdriver is not lined up in a north–south direction, hit the screwdriver with a hammer a few times. This will jumble the domains of iron molecules in the steel so that they will not line up in the same direction.

This is *not* the recommended way to demagnetize a watch.

DO NOT DEMAGNETIZE A WATCH LIKE THIS.

2. Heat the screwdriver until it is red hot, then let it cool slowly. Note: Be careful not to burn yourself or anyone else.

When you apply heat, the molecules in an object move rapidly. When you heat, then cool, a magnetized object, the molecules become jumbled and the force of magnetism is lost.

Once again, this is *not* the way to demagnetize a watch or other delicate instruments.

3. Make a coil of insulated electrical wire. Place the screwdriver blade or watch into the coil. Be care-

ful not to hurt yourself. Send an alternating current (see pages 97–98) through the wire. Cut the current very slowly, until it reaches zero. The alternating current jumbles the domains, causing the steel to be demagnetized.

This is the *recommended* way to demagnetize a watch.

THE EARTH'S MAGNETIC FIELD

In 1600 William Gilbert, an English doctor and physicist, performed a number of experiments regarding magnetism and published his findings in the book *De Magnete* (Concerning Magnets). Among his conclusions, Gilbert said that the earth itself acted as a huge magnet, just as though a huge bar magnet rested in the center of the earth.

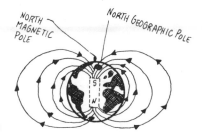

Gilbert's concept of the Earth's magnetic field

The imaginary bar magnet had its north pole (magnetic north) relatively near the geographic north pole (1500 miles away, somewhere in northern Canada) and the south pole (magnetic south) relatively near the geographic pole (1500 miles away).

The reason that the magnetic poles are called north and south is because they are in the general vicinity of the geographic poles.

A *compass* which is used to determine directions makes use of Gilbert's findings. It has a magnetic needle mounted on a horizontal plane (level with the ground) that turns freely on a pivot. The

**A compass can help guide
you through the woods.**

position of the north-seeking pole of the magnetic needle indicates the magnetic north.

Because the magnetic poles of the earth are not exactly the same as the geographic poles, compass needles

- in the western United States point several degrees east of true north.
- in the eastern United States point several degrees west of true north.

Magnetic north is not necessarily the same as true, geographic north.

If you were to use a compass in New York City, for example, the needle would point about 10° to 11° west of true geographic north.

A magnetic field can make a compass point in strange directions.

STATIC ELECTRICITY

Over 2,500 years ago Thales, a Greek philosopher and scientist, knew that if you rubbed a piece of amber (a yellowish fossil resin, like tree sap) with a cloth, the amber would attract pieces of dust and straw, much like a lodestone would attract bits of iron.

William Gilbert, the same scientist who discovered the earth's magnetic field in 1600, discovered that you could rub a variety of substances with a cloth and get the same attraction that you got by rubbing amber with a cloth. This attraction was called *electrification*, after the Greek word for amber, ελεκτρον (elektron).

In 1660 Otto van Guericke made a ball of sulphur and rotated it with a hand crank. He found that if he rubbed the ball with his hand while it rotated,

the ball would produce electrical sparks, and hold.
a static charge.

In 1706 Francis Hauksbee constructed a glass
ball, similar to Guericke's ball of sulphur. The glass
ball was able to hold a much larger static charge.

ELECTRICAL CHARGES

Under the proper circumstances, when two objects
are rubbed together, not only do they heat up due
to friction, but they also take on an *electric charge*.

Have you ever experienced a shock by walking
across a carpet and touching someone? If the an-

swer is yes, you've experienced static electricity
firsthand. Static electricity is an electrical charge
that rests on an object: your body, a comb, a balloon, even a magic wand.

Trick 4
The Card on the Wall
EFFECT: You take a selected card from the deck
and walk over to a wall. You then place the card on
the wall, where it sticks without falling down.

PROPS
    a deck of cards
    a room with carpeting

METHOD
This works best on a dry (nonhumid) day. Your shoes rubbing on the carpeting will build up a static charge on your body and on the card. When you place the card on the wall, it will stick because of static electricity.

Trick 5
The Balloon on the Wall
EFFECT: You rub a balloon on your head (bald magicians shouldn't try this trick), then place the balloon on the wall. The balloon sticks.

PROPS
    a balloon
    hair
    a wall

METHOD
By rubbing the balloon on your hair, you set up a static electricity charge on the balloon. The balloon sticks to the wall because of static electricity attraction, just like the card in the preceding trick.

NOTE: Magician Michael Chaut adds a new twist to this trick: He rubs the balloon on his head a number of times, yet the balloon won't stick to the wall. In reality, he just doesn't release the balloon when placing it on the wall.

After two or three attempts, Chaut rubs the balloon on his head, then makes believe that his head instead of the balloon is drawn to the wall and sticks there.

Trick 6
It Really is a Magic Wand

EFFECT: You read from a book. Rather than turning the pages with your hand, though, you simply hold a magic wand over the pages and command them to turn. They do.

PROPS
    a plastic magic wand
    a piece of cloth—silk, cotton, or wool
    a book

METHOD
The book is open on the table. The wand is rubbed with the cloth, setting up a static electricity charge. When the wand is brought near a page, the charge attracts the page.

**Static electricity can turn
the pages
of a magic book.**

With a little bit of practice, you can turn a page without touching the wand to the book.

Trick 7
The Dancing Slip O' Paper

EFFECT: You pass your magic wand over a piece of paper resting on the tabletop. The paper starts to move, finally stands up, then falls lifeless on the table.

PROPS
    a magic wand
    a piece of cloth—silk, wool, or cotton
    a piece of paper

METHOD
Rub the wand in one direction only with the cloth. This motion sets up a static charge on the wand that will attract the paper.

Try to rub the wand out of sight of your audience. If you must do it in front of them, complain about the "dust." Wipe off the "dust" with your cloth, really rubbing the wand to set up the charge.

NOTE: You can do this trick in a restaurant. Take a paper-wrapped straw and peel off the paper. Rub the straw with a cotton handkerchief or the bottom edge of your T-shirt. You can set up a static charge on the straw that will make the paper wrapper appear to dance on the table.

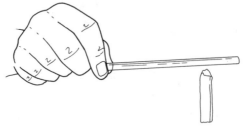

BENJAMIN FRANKLIN

It was known back in Benjamin Franklin's day that rubbing a hard rubber rod with a piece of wool flannel or fur, or rubbing a glass rod with a piece of silk, set up a static charge on the rod.

Franklin found that the charge on rubber was different from the charge on glass. From experiments, he learned that

- two charged rubber rods repelled each other
- two charged glass rods repelled each other
- a charged glass rod attracted a charged rubber rod

Franklin determined through his experiments that like charges (similar charges) repelled, unlike charges attracted. He called the charge from the glass rod positive (+) electricity, the charge from the rubber rod negative (−) electricity.

NOTE: Benjamin Franklin designated the charges plus and minus. Long before electrons were discovered, scientists assumed that electricity flowed from positive to negative. We now know that electrons flow from the negative side of a circuit to the positive side. Electricians still use the original, though incorrect, traditional direction of electrical flow from plus to minus.

ATOMS

Today, we know that the basic building blocks of elements, atoms, are made up of *subatomic particles*. The particles that we are interested in are called *electrons*, *protons*, and *neutrons*. The *nucleus* (central core) of all atoms contains *protons*. Protons have a positive charge. The nucleus of most atoms also contains neutrons. Neutrons have no charge. Surrounding the nucleus without touching it is a shell composed of *electrons*. Electrons have a negative charge.

Most atoms normally carry a *neutral* charge. This means that there are as many positive protons as negative electrons.

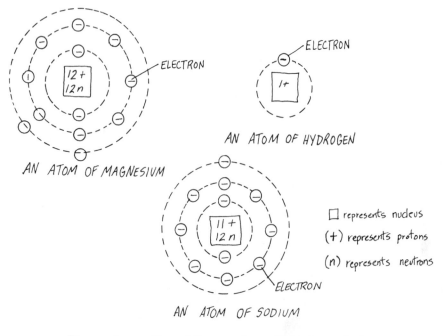

AN ATOM OF MAGNESIUM

AN ATOM OF HYDROGEN

AN ATOM OF SODIUM

☐ represents nucleus
(+) represents protons
(n) represents neutrons

Three atoms. Count the number of electrons (−) in each atom and compare them to the number of protons (+) in each nucleus.

We know that if you rub a plastic rod with a piece of cotton cloth, the cotton gives up a few electrons to the plastic rod. Because the cotton has fewer electrons, it now has a positive charge. This also means that the plastic rod now has a negative charge, because it has more electrons than protons.

We also know that if you rub a glass rod with silk, the glass gives up a few electrons to the silk. In this case, the glass has a positive charge.

Experiment 5
APPARATUS
>   a glass rod
>   2 plastic rods
>   a piece of silk and a piece of flannel
>   some thread or string
>   a thumbtack

PROCEDURE
Tie the string around the center of one plastic rod. Using the thumbtack, suspend the rod from the center of a doorway.

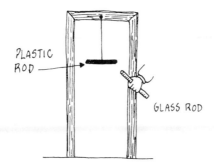

Charge the suspended plastic rod by rubbing it with the flannel. Charge the glass rod by rubbing it with the piece of silk. Try to touch the suspended plastic rod's end with the glass rod. What happens?

Charge the second plastic rod by rubbing it with the flannel. Try to touch the end of the hand-held plastic rod to the suspended plastic rod. What happens?

Charge the glass rod, then the plastic rod. Bring the two pieces of fabric near each other. What happens?

NOTE: Like charges repel, unlike charges attract, just like the north and south poles of magnets attracting or repelling each other.

INSULATING AND CONDUCTING

If an electrically charged body is to keep its charge, it must be *insulated* (kept away or isolated) from any material that allows the flow of electrons to or away from the charged body. A substance that allows the free flow of electrons is called a *conductor*. A substance that does not allow the free flow of electrons is an *insulator*.

If a charged plastic rod comes in contact with a conductor, the electrons leave the rod and flow to the conductor, covering its surface. If the charged plastic rod is insulated, it can hold a charge. If the conductor is not well insulated, it will lose its charge. In studying heat, we found out that anything that allowed the easy flow of heat was also called a conductor, a heat conductor. (See Book 3 on *Molecules and Heat*.)

Copper is a good conductor of both heat and electricity. If a conductor, such as copper, is connected to the ground (the earth), the conductor is said to be *grounded*. If a charged object is connected by a conductor to the ground, then the object loses its charge to the earth.

If the object's original charge was negative (that is, if it had more electrons than protons), then the electrons will usually travel through the conductor to the earth. If the object's original charge was positive (that is, if it had fewer electrons than protons), then the electrons will usually travel from the ground to the object.

Charges, both positive and negative, are stored in the massive charged body that we call the earth.

Static charges stay on the outside of conductors. A radio, TV, VCR, stereo, or other piece of electronic equipment is grounded to prevent the buildup of charges on the outside of the chassis (structure), which may interfere with proper operation.

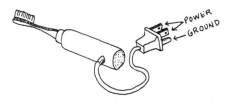

Electric toothbrushes are grounded to prevent you from getting a shock.

Experiment 6
APPARATUS
> 10 feet of insulated copper wire
> a plastic rod
> a piece of flannel
> some scraps of paper
> glue or tape

PROCEDURE

Before you do anything else, make sure that the plastic rod can be charged and can attract the scraps of paper (see Trick 7). After you have proven that the rod can be charged, remove about 1 foot of insulation from one end of the copper wire and wrap it around the plastic rod three or four times. (You can use glue or tape to hold the wire in place.) Attach the other end of the wire to a radiator or water pipe. Charge the plastic rod by rubbing it with the flannel. Then try to pick up the scraps of paper. What happens?

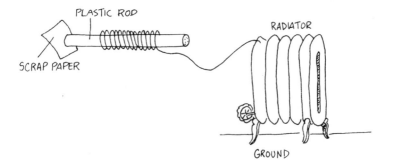

NOTE: The radiator or water pipe grounds the copper wire, and in turn the plastic rod. The copper wire allows the extra electrons generated from the rubbing action to flow away from the plastic rod to the radiator or water pipe, and then to the earth.

Materials that do not allow the free flow of electrons are called *insulators*. In the study of heat, we found that anything that prevented the flow of heat from one place to another was also called an insulator.

Experiment 7

APPARATUS

   10 feet of insulated copper wire
   a plastic rod 12 inches long
   a piece of rubber tubing
   a piece of flannel
   some scraps of paper
   glue or tape

PROCEDURE

Put the rubber tube (insulation) around the last three inches of the plastic rod.

   Before you do anything else, make sure that the plastic rod can still be charged and can attract the scraps of paper. After you have proven that the rod can be charged, remove about 1 foot of insulation from one end of the copper wire and wrap it around the rubber tubing three or four times. (You can use glue or tape to hold it in place.) Attach the other end of the wire to a radiator or water pipe. Charge the plastic rod by rubbing it with the flannel. Then try to pick up the scraps of paper. What happens?

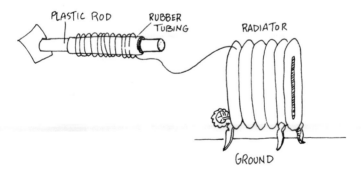

PLASTIC ROD   RUBBER TUBING   RADIATOR

GROUND

NOTE: The rubber tubing should insulate the charged rod from the copper wire, which leads to the radiator or water pipe (the ground). If the rod is insulated, it should be able to hold a charge and attract scraps of paper.

MORE BENJAMIN FRANKLIN

Benjamin Franklin performed a famous experiment in 1752 that proved that lightning was an electrical discharge. The experiment was very dangerous, even though Franklin didn't realize it at the time.

DON'T ATTEMPT TO DUPLICATE THIS EXPERIMENT.
YOU WILL BE BADLY HURT.

Franklin flew a kite during a thunderstorm. The kite was attached to silken thread that led to Franklin's hand via a cotton thread. Attached to the silk thread was a brass key.

After a short time, Franklin attempted to touch the brass key with his knuckles. A spark filled the gap between the key and his knuckles, proving to Franklin, and the world, that lightning was a discharge of static electricity.

Franklin believed that when a building was struck by lightning, the air around it had a positive charge and the building a negative charge brought about by the action of the storm. If a needle of iron were attached to the top of the building and grounded, any charge that built up in the air over the building would be quickly neutralized by the conductor leading into the ground.

Franklin had invented the *lightning rod*, which proved effective in preventing lightning from striking buildings.

More about lightning later.

"DANGEROUS, DO NOT DO THIS."

INDUCTION 1

By approaching a neutrally charged, insulated object with a charged rod, you can induce a charge in the insulated body without actually touching it.

One machine that you might find in a laboratory that works on this principle is the the Van de Graaff generator. It is an electro-static generator. It is used to study the effects of static electricity and may even be used for "atom smashing" experiments.

Perhaps you've been to a science museum that had one of these generators on display. The instructor may have had a volunteer place one hand on the ball of the machine. When the machine was switched on, the volunteer's hair stood on end.

The electrostatic generator put a charge on the body of the volunteer. Since all of the charge was

Touching a Van de Graaff generator can be a hair-raising experience.

◆ 55 ◆

the same (either positive or negative), each charged hair on the volunteer's head tried to move away from the hair next to it.

Back in the section on magnetism, we learned that there was something called a magnetic field surrounding magnets. In the study of electricity, we find an *electric field* surrounding charged objects.

In studying magnets, we learned that like fields repelled and unlike fields attracted. In studying electric fields, we also find that like charges repel and unlike charges attract.

The electric fields can be mapped as we did with magnetic fields (see Experiment 3). Electric fields are similar in appearance to magnetic fields.

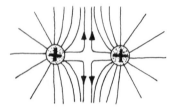

THE REPULSION OF LIKE CHARGES   THE ATTRACTION OF UNLIKE CHARGES

POTENTIAL DIFFERENCE

In the third book in this series, we discussed potential energy. If a ball is resting on a windowsill 25 feet (7.62 m) above the ground and rolls off, the potential energy at 25 feet is converted to kinetic energy at ground level.

Another way of saying that is the ball went from a site of higher potential energy (the windowsill) to a site of lower potential energy (the ground). We can say that there was a *potential difference* between

the ball when it was on the windowsill and when it finally reached the ground.

The same concept can be applied to water. In studying fluids, we find that water seeks its own level. The surface is not bumpy, but smooth. The reason is that gravity pulls equally on molecules of

Water seeks its own level as it flows down a mountainside.

water, which gives the entire body of water a smooth surface. The molecules of water in a mountainside stream must flow downhill until the pull of gravity is equalized, when the water reaches a lake or ocean. We can say that there is a *potential difference* between the water on the top of the mountain and the water in the lake.

We can say the same thing when we charge an object. A charge "wants to" move if there is a *potential difference* between the place where the charge is and the place that it wants to go. If you have two metal objects with a potential difference, the charge "wants to" flow from the place of high charge to the place of low charge. If the potential difference is great enough, the charge will flow through the air in the form of a spark or lightning bolt.

The higher the charge on an insulated conductor, the higher the potential difference. The amount of charge that a conductor can hold is known as its electrical *capacitance* (electrical capacity). These kinds of devices are found in radios, TVs, VCRs, etc. They are called *capacitors*. Capacitors are able to store up an electrical charge. Sometimes, when you turn a radio or TV off, it continues to play for a few seconds. The reason for this is that the capacitors take a few seconds to lose their charge.

If you ever take apart a radio or TV, you must be careful. If you accidentally discharge a capacitor, you may be in for a terrible shock.

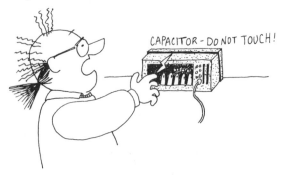

Today we know that electrical charges are built up in a thunder (cumulonimbus) cloud. A cloud of this type usually has a strong updraft of air at the center. Raindrops falling through the updraft create friction by moving against the air. The action of the friction gives a negative charge to large raindrops (just as you do to a plastic rod when you rub it with a piece of silk or flannel). The air molecules and smaller, misty drops of water are positively charged as they are carried by the updraft toward the top of the cloud. Sometimes the top and bottom of the cloud are separated by a neutrally charged layer of air, creating a large cloud capacitor.

A lightning bolt may strike in the sky when two clouds of opposite charge get near each other. A

lightning bolt may strike the ground when a low-hanging cloud with a negative charge induces a large positive charge in something on the ground. Once the potential difference is large enough, lightning strikes and BOOM!

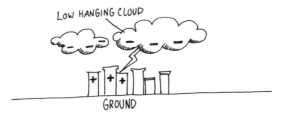

LOW HANGING CLOUD

GROUND

ELECTRICAL CURRENT

In a river, the flow of water is called a current. In a solid, such as copper wire, the flow or movement of electrons is called an *electrical current*. In a river,

the water molecules flow from a higher point to a lower point, being pulled by gravity. In a closed hydraulic system, like an automobile's cooling sys-

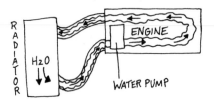

tem, the fluid flows from an area of high pressure to an area of low pressure. In a wire, electrons usually flow from an area of negative charge to an area of positive charge.

The following pages will discuss why and how the electrons flow.

MEASUREMENT OF CURRENT

When we measure the flow of water, we measure the amount of water passing a point in a certain amount of time, such as gallons or liters per second. When we measure the flow of electricity, we measure the amount of electrons passing a point in a certain amount of time.

We measure the flow of electricity in the unit called the *ampere* (*amp* for short), named for the French physicist André-Marie Ampère.

NOTE: In 1820 Ampère discovered that wires carrying electrical currents could develop magnetic properties.

An ampere, then, is the amount of charge passing a given point in a given time. One ampere equals 6,280,000,000,000,000,000 (6.28

$\times 10^{18}$) electrons passing a given point in one second.

The amount of charge in 6.28×10^{18} electrons equals 1 *coulomb*. Charge is the amount of extra electrons or extra protons on a body. The coulomb is the standard measurement of charge used by most scientists and engineers today.

There are so many electrons crowded together in copper wire that they move very slowly, about $\frac{1}{100}$ of an inch a second. If 6.28×10^{18} electrons can pass a point in one second while moving only $\frac{1}{100}$ of an inch, you can imagine how tiny the electrons are.

You might ask, "If electrons move so slowly, how come the light bulb in my room lights up as soon as

I hit the switch?" This happens because electrons jam the wires conducting electricity, much more crowded than passengers in a subway car during rush hour or sardines in a can.

The light goes on for the same reason that water comes out of your kitchen faucet when you turn it on: The pipe to the faucet is always filled with water and the wire is always filled with electrons. When the water faucet is opened, the water in the pipe that was held back by the closed faucet comes pouring out. The electrical wires coming into your house are always filled with electrons. The wires from the switch to the light bulb are always filled with electrons. When the switch is opened, the electrons move from one side of the switch to the other.

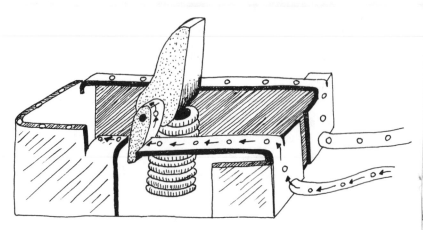

BATTERIES

A battery keeps electrons flowing in a wire, in much the same way that a water pump keeps water flowing in an automobile system.

In an automobile cooling system, the water pump pushes the coolant through a hose into the radiator, then into the engine block, then back to the water pump. The pump moves the water by causing an increase in pressure at the water pump outlet and a decrease in pressure at the water pump inlet.

A battery works in pretty much the same way, only with electrons instead of water. We call the difference in pressure between the *anode* (positive terminal) and the *cathode* (negative terminal) the *PD* (potential difference). The PD keeps the electrons flowing.

A flashlight's electrons flow when the switch is closed.

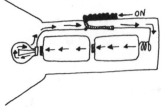

**The electron flow ceases
when the switch
is opened.**

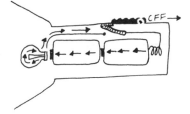

HISTORICAL BACKGROUND

In 1780 the Italian biologist Luigi Galvani found that the muscles of a dead frog's leg would twitch if they were zapped by an electric spark.

Galvani knew about Benjamin Franklin's experiments with lightning (see page 54). To test the effects of electricity on animal tissue, he hung frog legs on brass hooks outside his window during an electrical storm. The legs started twitching even though there was no lightning.

Galvani investigated and found that the frog legs were touching ornamental ironwork around the

window, as well as the brass hooks. He later discovered that the legs would twitch whenever they were in contact with two different metals. Galvani thought that the electricity causing the twitching was created in the muscles of the frog legs. He called it "animal electricity."

Twenty years later in 1800, Alessandro Guiseppe Volta, an Italian scientist, found out that an electric current was produced when *any two dissimilar metals* were in contact with each other. Frog legs were unnecessary except as a delicacy in France.

Volta conducted many tests with electricity. In one experiment, he placed a number of bowls of saltwater next to each other, then linked the bowls with arched strips of metal. One end of each strip was copper, the other end was zinc or tin. He called the result an *electric battery*.

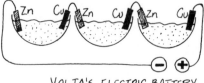

VOLTA'S ELECTRIC BATTERY

NOTE: A battery is a series of similar items working together as a single unit.

Volta's battery generated a current of electricity rather than static (standing still) electricity.

Volta then condensed the battery into a smaller unit by forming a "sandwich" of small discs, all moistened with saltwater. The disc sandwich (not exactly lunch) was made of layers of copper, zinc, and cardboard. When Volta attached a wire to the top and bottom of the battery, a current flowed. A single unit of this type of battery is called a *voltaic cell*, named for Volta.

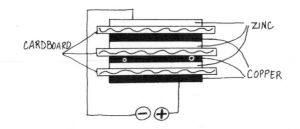

It was a great invention, but, unfortunately for Volta, portable radios had not yet been invented and he didn't have much to do with his battery—except make frog legs twitch.

Only seven weeks after Volta proved that electric current could be generated from a chemical reaction (copper and zinc reacting with the saltwater), a British scientist, William Nicholson, passed an electric current from a battery like Volta's through water (H_2O). The result that Nicholson achieved was a breakdown of the water into its fundamental parts, hydrogen and oxygen. Nicholson's experiment showed that an electric current could give rise to a chemical reaction.

The problem with batteries like Volta's was that after a short while the batteries stopped working. This was because the chemicals causing the electrical reaction were soon used up. This problem was

solved in 1859 by the French scientist Gaston Plante. Plante separated two sheets of lead with a rubber sheet, rolled them into a spiral coil, and placed them in a solution of sulfuric acid. Not only did he get an electric current from this new battery, but when the battery ran down, he could force an electric current back into it, reversing the chemical

reaction and allowing the battery to once again produce electricity. Pictured here is a simple voltaic
cell. Hydrochloric acid is formed when hydrogen
chloride mixes with water. The hydrogen chloride
separates into a hydrogen part and a chlorine part
when dissolved in water. When these parts separate,
the chlorine atom has an extra electron attached to it,
which gives it a negative (−) charge. The hydrogen
atom is missing an electron and has a positive (+)
charge. These charged atoms are called *ions*.

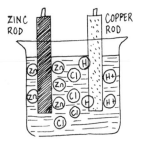

The atoms of zinc tend to dissolve in the acid.
Each time an atom of zinc goes into solution, it
leaves two electrons on the zinc rod, giving the zinc
a negative (−) charge. Since the atoms of zinc in
solution are missing two electrons, they have a positive (+) charge. The zinc ions with a positive (+)
charge repel the positively charged hydrogen ions.
The hydrogen ions accumulate around the copper
rod.

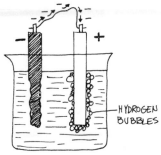

When a connection is made between the copper rod and the negatively charged zinc rod with a piece of wire, all of the extra electrons on the zinc rod move over the connecting wire and down the copper rod and merge with the positively charged hydrogen ions. Once a hydrogen ion merges with an electron, it becomes an ordinary hydrogen atom, floats to the top of the acid around the copper rod, and finally leaves the liquid. This reaction occurs until the zinc rod is totally dissolved.

Betcha 2
"I betcha that I can light up this electric bulb with a lemon."

PROPS
> a small flashlight bulb
> a lemon
> a strip of zinc
> a strip of copper

PROCEDURE
Cut a small hole in the skin of the lemon. Insert the zinc strip about 1 to 2 inches into the lemon. Push one end of the copper into the lemon. *Don't* let the copper touch the zinc. Put the base of the bulb on the zinc. Touch the copper to the threads around the base of the bulb. The bulb should light up.

NOTE: You have constructed a small battery. The copper and zinc are dissimilar metals. The lemon juice is an acid, and a chemical reaction is taking place in the lemon, in a fashion similar to the voltaic cell explained in the preceding pages.

There are two types of electric batteries: primary and secondary cells. In a *primary cell*, the electricity-producing chemicals are used up and the cell cannot be recharged. This is the kind of battery you'll usually find in a toy, game, or personal stereo.

A *secondary cell* can be recharged. The chemicals in a secondary cell are used up as the battery drains, but they are recharged when an electric current is passed through them. Rechargeable batteries for home use are usually of the ni-cad (nickel-cadmium) type. Another type of rechargeable battery is found in automobiles, boats, and motorcycles. These are wet cell batteries that require acid to work properly.

DRY CELLS

The average dry cell battery has a PD (potential difference) of about 1½ volts.

If you hooked up dry cell batteries together positive to negative, the potential difference would equal

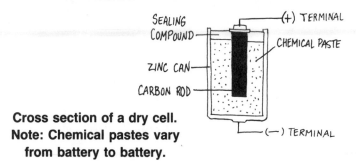

**Cross section of a dry cell.
Note: Chemical pastes vary
  from battery to battery.**

1½ volts times the number of batteries. Batteries hooked up in such a manner are said to be *in series*.

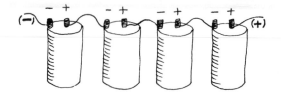

WET CELLS

Wet cell batteries are the type invented by Gaston Plante. In general, in a wet cell the two metals used are lead and lead peroxide. They usually sit in a bath of sulfuric acid (H_2SO_4). These metals don't dissolve like the zinc rod in the voltaic cell described earlier (see page 65).

A wet cell battery can be recharged by passing an electric current through it. In a car, the battery is charged by an alternator, a type of generator that produces alternating current. (For more information on generators, see pages 95–96. For more information on alternating current, see pages 97–98.)

ELEMENTARY CIRCUITRY

A *circuit* is the complete path of an electric current. We can make a simple circuit by connecting a battery to a flashlight bulb, just as we did in Betcha 2, but instead we'll try it with a regular battery.

Experiment 8
APPARATUS
   2 pieces of flexible insulated copper wire, each 12 inches (30.77 cm) long
   a dry cell battery—a Lantern cell with screw posts

a flashlight bulb

a bulb socket to fit the bulb (you can find all of the above in an electronics supply store, such as Radio Shack)

a piece of wood 12 × 12 × 1 inch (30.77 × 30.77 × 2.56 cm)

PROCEDURE

Strip the insulation from the ends of the two pieces of wire. Attach the bulb socket to the piece of wood. Attach the ends of the wires to the bulb socket. Attach the wires to the battery's screw posts. The light should glow. You have completed a circuit.

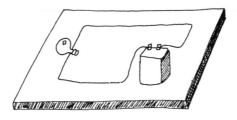

A simple circuit

NOTE: The side of the battery with the greater amount of electrons (the negative side) pushes those electrons down the wire through the bulb and back to the battery.

This will continue until you disconnect the battery from the circuit or the battery runs out of electrochemical power. (Electrochemical power is the electrical power that is stored in the chemicals of a battery.)

In this experiment you created a flashlight. This flashlight isn't the easiest to carry around, but it works in the same way as a typical household flashlight.

Experiment 9

APPARATUS

   the apparatus from Experiment 8
   2½-inch (1.3-cm) flat-headed nails
   a piece of aluminum 3 × ½ inch (7.7 × 1.3 cm)
cut from a soda can.

Be very careful when cutting the soda can. The edges of the metal can be very sharp. Have an adult help you.

PROCEDURE

Disconnect the wires to the battery. Cut one of the wires in half. Strip ½ inch (1.3 cm) of insulation from the wire's new ends. Wrap the end of this wire around one nail and hammer the nail into the wood.

   Measure and mark 2½ inches (6.4 cm) from the nail head on the wood. Place one end of the aluminum on the mark you just made and the other end on the head of the nail in the wood. Wrap the end of the other wire around the nail. Hammer the second nail through the strip of aluminum and into the wood. Bend the piece of aluminum so that it can touch only the second nail when you press down on it. Attach the free ends of the wire to the battery's terminal.

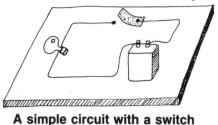

A simple circuit with a switch

NOTE: In this experiment, the piece of aluminum acts as a *switch*. A switch is a movable contact that allows the free flow of electrons when closed and stops the flow of electrons when open. When you press down on the piece of aluminum so that it is in contact with both nail heads, the circuit is closed. This means that the electric current is conducted and the bulb will light up. When you release the aluminum, the circuit is open. This means that the electric current is stopped and the bulb will stop glowing.

RESISTANCE

In 1827 Georg Simon Ohm, a German scientist, discovered that the length and thickness (cross section) of materials made a difference in the amount of electricity flowing in a circuit.

DEFINITELY NOT OHM'S LAW

He stated, "The flow of current through a conductor is directly proportional to the potential difference and inversely proportional to the resistance." This means that if you *increase* the potential difference, you *increase* the *flow* of electricity. If you *decrease* the potential difference, you *decrease* the *flow* of electricity.

If you *increase* the *resistance* in a circuit, you *decrease* the *flow* of electricity. If you *decrease* the *resistance* in a circuit, you *increase* the *flow* of electricity.

Experiment 10
APPARATUS

the apparatus from Experiment 8

a thick pencil lead from a mechanical pencil

2 pieces of flexible insulated copper wire, each 12 inches (30.77 cm) long

2½-inch (1.3-cm) flat-headed nails

a 3 × ½ inch (7.7 by 1.3 cm) piece of aluminum from a soda can

PROCEDURE

Set up another circuit on the wooden board from Experiment 8. Once the second circuit is complete, cut one wire in half and strip the insulation from the ends. Wrap the ends of the wire around the ends of the pencil lead. Close the new circuit and note how brightly the bulb glows. Open the new circuit, close the original circuit, and notice the brightness of the bulb.

Graphite has more resistance than copper. The light bulb will not be as bright as the previous circuit.

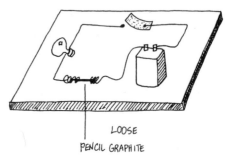

LOOSE
PENCIL GRAPHITE

NOTE: The bulb glows more brightly in the original circuit. The new circuit has a greater resistance due to the pencil lead (actually graphite, a compound of carbon and clay). Carbon conducts electricity, but not as well as copper wire. Therefore, the bulb does not glow as brightly in the second circuit, which uses carbon.

Experiment 11
APPARATUS
the apparatus from Experiment 10

PROCEDURE
Unwrap one wire from one end of the pencil lead. Close the switch in the circuit. Run the loose wire end up and down the length of the pencil lead. The closer you move the unconnected wire to the connected wire, the brighter the bulb glows. The farther away you move the unconnected wire, the dimmer the bulb becomes.

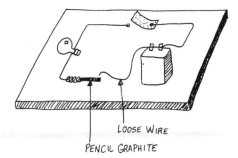

LOOSE WIRE

PENCIL GRAPHITE

Touching the loose wire to the graphite, the closer you get to the wire-wrapped end, the brighter the light because there is less resistance.

NOTE: Again, the pencil lead (or graphite) affects the amount of resistance, and thus the current.

- Less pencil lead between the ends of the wire = less resistance = more current.
- More pencil lead between the ends of the wire = greater resistance = less current.

Trick 8
The Lie Detector

> YOU SHOULD HAVE AN ADULT WHO KNOWS SOMETHING ABOUT ELECTRONICS HELP WITH THE CONSTRUCTION OF THIS DEVICE.

EFFECT: The magician displays a plastic box and tells the audience that it is a lie detector. There is a push-button switch on top of the box and a piece of string coming from a small hole in the side of the box. The magician explains that when a lie is told, the box buzzes, then pushes the button on top to demonstrate the buzz.

LIE DETECTOR

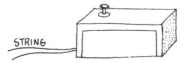

OUTSIDE VIEW

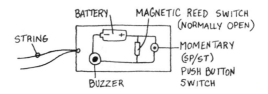

INSIDE VIEW

The magician has a spectator hold the string and places the plastic box on the tabletop. The magician now asks the spectator questions such as:

- How old are you?
- What color hair do you have?
- Do you cheat on tests?
- Do you have a friend named Johann Nepomuk Hofsinzer?

The buzzer, which is under your control, sounds.

PROPS
> a plastic box, with a locking cover, big enough to hold the following:
> a 9-volt buzzer
> a 9-volt battery and battery holder
> a small push-button "momentary on" switch
> a mini "normally open" magnetic reed switch
> a spool of insulated electronic wire (22 gauge)
> solder and soldering iron
> **NOTE:** Most of this stuff will be found in a Radio Shack or other electronics store
> a piece of string
> a small powerful magnet
> an Ace® bandage
> glue or tape

CONSTRUCTION
Drill a hole in the plastic box and install the switch.

Before you can solder wire to switches, you must strip about ½ inch (1.3 cm) of insulation from the ends of the wire. To do this, very carefully cut the insulation around the wire with a sharp knife. Be careful not to cut through the wire or cut your fingers. Grasp the insulation with pliers and gently pull it off.

Connect two lengths of wire to the switch's contacts and solder them in place. Attach one of the wires to one terminal on the battery holder. Attach a third length of wire to the same terminal on the battery holder. Attach the reed switch to the third wire.

Attach the free ends of the wires from both the reed switch and the push-button switch to one terminal of the buzzer. Attach a length of wire to the second terminal of the buzzer and the free terminal of the battery holder. Insert the battery into the holder and put all of this circuitry into the box. Make sure that the reed switch stays on the bottom of the box. Secure it in place with glue or tape.

Drill a small hole in the box and thread the string through it. Tie a knot on both ends of the string so it can't be pulled out of the box. The string is just a prop. (It does nothing, but it helps to convince your audience that this device really is a lie detector.) Place the cover on the box.

METHOD

Secure the magnet to your knee with the Ace® bandage. When the box is on the table, you should be able to position the magnet directly below it. The magnetic field should be strong enough to penetrate the table and the plastic box. The magnetic field will close the ordinarily open magnetic reed switch. When that occurs the buzzer will go off.

The circuit you have constructed has two switches: the push-button and the reed. You may want to experiment with the reed switch before you put it in the box. If you listen carefully, you can hear it close when the magnet is brought near it and open when the magnet is taken away.

NOTE: A similar type of switch is used in burglar alarm systems. The switch in such a system, though, is a little larger and a little more conspicuous. If you're interested, check out this type of switch at any electronics supply store.

Trick 9
The Pencil Radio

YOU SHOULD HAVE AN ADULT WHO KNOWS SOMETHING ABOUT ELECTRON-ICS HELP WITH THE CONSTRUCTION OF THIS DEVICE.

EFFECT: You show a pencil to your friends and say to them, "This is really a radio. Would you like to hear it?" When they say yes, pantomime twisting the eraser as if to turn on the radio. Suddenly it starts to play.

PROPS
A small portable radio with a built-in speaker; this should be a radio that you have no other use for and you are willing to dedicate to this trick. The radio must be gimmicked with a special switch that is described below.

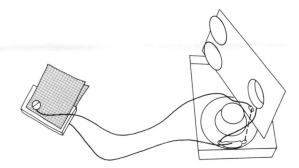

To make the switch, you need:
2 pieces of 18-gauge insulated copper wire
2 pieces of brass strip ½ × 2 inches (1.28 × 5.13 cm) (available from hobby or hardware stores)
a piece of cardboard ½ × ½ inch (1.28 × 1.28 cm)
a hot melt glue gun
a soldering iron with solder

PREPARATION

The first thing that you must do is make a "belly switch." Solder one wire to the end of one brass strip. Solder the other wire to the second brass strip. Follow the diagram to see the construction of the switch.

Place cardboard between the two brass strips, near the ends with the wires. Glue the cardboard and brass strips together with the hot melt glue gun.

Now insert the switch in the radio. (You should be careful with this next step or you might ruin the radio and the trick will not work.) First, open up the back of the radio, remove the batteries, and find the two wires that run to the speaker. Cut one of those wires in half. Strip each end of insulation for about one quarter inch. Next, solder one wire from your "belly switch" to one of the speaker wire's cut ends and the switch's other wire to the speaker wire's other cut end. Finally, replace the batteries and close the radio's case, letting the wires snake through the case's seam.

At this point, you should turn the radio on by the normal switch, squeeze the belly switch closed, tune in a station, and adjust the volume. Once the station is tuned in, stop squeezing the belly switch. The radio should stop playing.

Now, for the moment of truth.

NOTE: Brass strips are used because they have a little bit of natural spring. If they tend to touch each other, just put a small bend in one, so it arcs away from the other.

METHOD

Make sure that you're wearing a pair of pants that need a belt and a jacket or vest. The radio should be inside your shirt, hidden underneath your jacket or vest. The switch should be between your waist and your belt. You should adjust the belt so that it is tight enough to hold your pants up but loose enough to avoid squeezing the switch.

Proceed with the trick as stated in Effect. When the time comes to "play" the pencil, push out your stomach, squeezing the switch against the belt. That squeeze should be enough to close the switch, which closes the circuit, allowing the pencil to play, just like a radio.

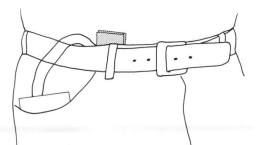

The positioning of the belly switch. The radio can be under your shirt or jacket or in your pants' pocket.

NOTE: When you let your friends listen to the pencil, you hold on to it and position it directly in front of the hidden radio. If you practice this and perform it well, your friends will never suspect how you do it.

Trick 10
Find the Switch
EFFECT: The magician, that's you, brings out a little plastic box. On top of the box is a small light bulb and three push-button switches. You patter about this being a computerized version of an old guessing game. "Only if you know how to play, it's never a guess."

You push a switch a few times and the light goes on and off. After a while, you let your spectator try to light the switch. He is never successful, while you always are.

PROPS
    a small plastic box with a lid
    3 push-button single-pole/double-throw switches (available at good hardware stores)
    a 9-volt battery and battery holder (Radio Shack)
    a 5-volt LED (light-emitting diode) from Radio Shack
    silicone sealing glue

SETUP
Drill 4 holes in the top of the box, as shown in the illustration. Insert the switches and light-emitting diode in the appropriate holes. Glue the LED in place with silicone sealing glue. Secure the switches in place with their attaching washers and nuts.

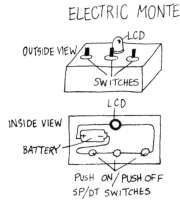

ELECTRIC MONTE

OUTSIDE VIEW — LCD — SWITCHES

INSIDE VIEW — LCD — BATTERY

PUSH ON / PUSH OFF
SP/DT SWITCHES

Connect the switches, LED, and battery holder in *series*. (See illustration.) Insert the battery. Close the box. Try to light the LED.

First, hit the switches in 1—2—3 order. Then 3—2—1. Then 2—1—3. Eventually, the bulb will light up and you're ready to perform this trick.

METHOD

Looking at the box the same way all the time is a big help. Mentally label the switches A—B—C. Once the bulb is on, press button C, turning the LED off. Say to your friend, "When I push this switch," push button C, "the LED lights." "When I push it again, it goes off." Do so. "The whole purpose of this game is to light the LED." Push button B twice, and say, "This button does nothing." Push button A once. Say, "Nor does this button."

NOTE: Right now, both end buttons A and C are off. As you hand the box over, you say, "Just hit the end button." Nothing happens. You say, "I meant the other one." Push that button and the bulb lights. Then you press the button that you just pressed one more time and the LED goes out.

Press button C twice. The first time the LED lights, the second time it goes out. Next show that buttons B and A do nothing. Push them once each. Ask your friend to press an end button. No matter which one he presses, nothing happens. Have him push the other one. Still nothing. You press the middle button once and the LED lights.

The instructions sound confusing, but if you construct this item and practice it while reading the instructions, you will have a lot of fun with it.

NOTE: You have constructed a very simple circuit of three switches in *series* with an LED and battery. All three of the switches have to be in a closed position (allowing electricity to flow) for the LED to light. If any combination of the switches is open, the LED will not light. When you or your friend press the switches, you must keep in mind which switches are open and closed.

(This trick was invented by Jerry Lubin and sold in magic shops prior to the publication of Lubin's pamphlet, *My Favorite Pastime*, in 1970.)

ELECTRICITY AND HEAT

A by-product of electricity is heat. When electrons move through a circuit, they constantly bang into atoms. This motion causes heat. The faster the flow of electrons, the greater the heat. The greater the resistance, the greater the heat.

Sometimes heat is an unwanted by-product. Examples of unwanted heat occur in computers, VCRs, TVs, and electric motors. That's why many of these

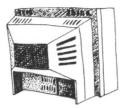

items have ventilating holes and fans built in to draw in cool air, helping to get rid of excess heat.

In other applications we find the heat useful:

a) An incandescent light bulb uses a filament with very high resistance. The temperature gets so high in a light bulb that the filament starts to glow, creating light.

b) Electric arcs create high temperatures and bright light. They are used in certain types of movie projectors and industrial ovens for melting metal. They are also used for arc welding.

c) Electrically generated heat is the basis for such products as toasters, electric blankets, coffee makers, heating pads, and automobile rear window defrosters.

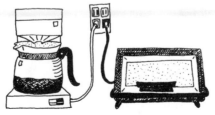

When using electricity, we have to be careful for a few reasons. One of the reasons is that the greater the amount of current drawn by an appliance, the greater the amount of heat generated. If there is too much current, the wire's insulation may burn or melt away. In these instances, there is a strong possibility of a fire.

To counteract the overloading of circuits, we use fuses and circuit breakers. A fuse is a piece of metal that has a high resistance and a low melting point. If too much current is going through the circuit, the fuse will get hot and then melt, breaking the circuit. In the average house, a fuse is good for between 15 and 20 amps (remember Ampère? page 60). Fuses in electronic components look different from household fuses, but work in the same way. Too much current and they blow.

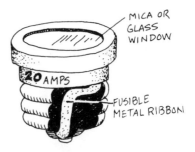

ELECTROMAGNETISM

In 1820 the Swedish scientist Hans Christian Θersted made his discoveries regarding electro-magnetism public. As noted before in this book, electric currents exhibit magnetic field properties. They both have north poles and south poles. The charges (+ & −) that electric currents generate also behave like magnetic fields. Like charges repel and unlike charges attract.

**This levitating globe floats
due to electromagnetism.**

Θersted found through experimentation that the needle of a compass brought near a wire with an electric current flowing through it would point at right angles to the flow of the current. If the current went from north to south, the needle of the compass pointed east to west. If the current reversed and flowed from south to north, the needle of the compass would reverse itself and point west to east.

The oersted, the unit of magnetic field strength, is named for him.

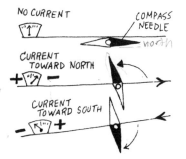

Experiment 12
APPARATUS
>   a Lantern battery (like that used in Experiment 8)
>   1 24-inch (6.09 dm) long piece of 18 gauge wire
>   a magnetic compass

PROCEDURES
Bend the wire into a big loop. Attach the ends of the wire to the screw posts on the battery. Place the compass at different points on the loop of wire. Then place it beneath, on each side of, and on top of the wire at various points. Notice that, no matter where the compass is placed, the needle stays at right angles to the wire.

Reverse the wire's ends on the screw posts. What happens to the needle of the compass?

Experiment 13
PROPS
>   a Lantern battery (see Experiment 12)
>   1 wire 24 inches (6.09 dm) long
>   a magnetic compass
>   a piece of cardboard
>   some iron filings

PROCEDURE

Punch a small hole in the center of the cardboard. Pass one end of the wire through the hole. Connect each end of the wire to the battery terminal.

Slowly sprinkle iron filings on top of the cardboard. Notice how the filings form a pattern. This pattern proves that a magnetic field has been established around the wire. The magnetic field's lines of force are arranged in concentric circles, with the wire in the center.

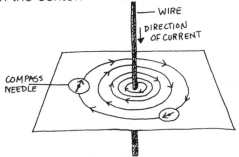

MORE HISTORY

The French physicist Ampère conducted additional experiments in electricity and magnetism. He discovered that two parallel wires carrying current flowing in the same direction attracted each other. If the current flowed in opposite directions, though, the wires repelled each other.

Ampere's observation of current-bearing wires

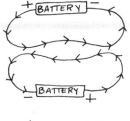

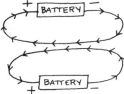

A German scientist named Johann Schweigger discovered that the amount of current flowing through a wire could be measured with a compass by observing the amount of deflection in the compass's needle. This was the basis of the gauge that we know today as a *galvanometer*, named to honor Luigi Galvani.

Johann Schweigger's observation

Ampère also wrapped some wire in a helix (corkscrew or spiral), called a *solenoid*, and passed a current through the wire. The wire attracted iron filings.

In 1823 the English scientist William Sturgeon developed the electromagnet. He wrapped a helix of eighteen turns around a soft iron core, then passed a current through the wire. Sturgeon discovered that the iron core strengthened the wire's magnetic field.

In 1829 the American physicist Joseph Henry improved on Sturgeon's electromagnet by wrapping hundreds of coils around an iron core. With this simple magnet and a powerful battery, Henry was able to lift over a ton of iron.

Electromagnets are used today in telephones, loudspeakers, doorbells, buzzers, and automobile

I INVENTED THE ELECTROMAGNET.

I IMPROVED IT.

I GOT THEM BOTH BEAT.

AMPERE

STURGEON

HENRY

starters. When the button is pushed to ring a household bell, the circuit is closed. The electrons activate an electromagnet, which moves the bell's clapper to strike the bell. As the clapper moves, the circuit is broken and a spring brings the clapper back to the starting position, where the cycle is repeated again and again until the button is released.

INDUCTION 2

Much of the early work in the fields of electricity, electrochemistry, and electromagnetism was done by Michael Faraday, an English scientist. In one of his experiments, Faraday hooked up a coil of wire to a meter. When he approached the coil with either pole of a bar magnet, a short-lived electric current was produced. When he removed the magnet from the area of the coil, another short-lived current was produced.

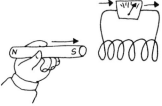

Faraday found that he could strengthen the current by (a) increasing the strength of the magnet, (b) increasing the number of turns in the coil, or (c) speeding up the movement of the magnet. He also discovered that if the coil and meter circuit (let's call this circuit 2) was next to another circuit (let's call this circuit 1), a momentary current was started in circuit 2 when a current flow was started or stopped in circuit 1.

Faraday noticed that the current flow in circuit 2 was in one direction when circuit 1 was closed (started) and in the opposite direction when circuit 1 was opened (stopped).

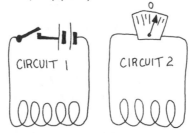

Currents of electricity are produced when magnetic lines of force cut across conductive wires. These electric currents are caused by *electromagnetic induction*.

ELECTRIC MOTORS

In 1821 Faraday discovered that an electric current could produce mechanical motion. One of the circuits that he designed included a wire that could move around a magnet. When he passed a current through the wire, the wire revolved around the magnet. Faraday discovered that when a wire with a current running through it (a current-bearing wire) is placed in a magnetic field, a sideward force is produced that attempts to push the wire out of the magnetic field.

Faraday was the first scientist to suggest that magnets have *lines of force* coming from them. A current-bearing wire has lines of force that arrange themselves in concentric circles around the wire. See Experiment 13. These concentric lines of force allow the wire to turn. A coil of wire with a current flowing through it, turning continuously in a magnetic field due to the force, is called an electric motor.

The magnetic field of the wire coil is repelled by the magnetic field of the magnets and pushed out of the field. If there was a solid wire connection, the wires would become twisted and cease turning after a few revolutions. To allow an electric motor to turn, we need to have a sliding contact between the wire

Magnetic fields will affect electrical fields.

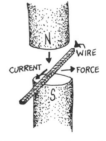

coil and the power source. This contact on the coil is called a *commutator*. The power is transferred to the commutator by sliding contacts called *brushes*. The commutator is usually split in half so that the electric current is always flowing in the proper direction. This is known as a *split ring commutator*.

A basic electric motor

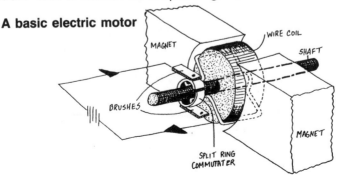

Experiment 14
A Simple Motor
(based on an idea of Rudy Keil)
APPARATUS
    a C cell battery
    a small ceramic magnet (the kind used to deco-
rate refrigerators)
    hot-melt glue
    5 feet (1.52 m) of #22 enameled copper wire
    2 copper paper clips
    rubber bands
    sandpaper

PREPARATION
Wrap the wire around the battery about ten times,
forming a coil. Remove the coil and set it aside.

    Straighten the paper clips, then bend them with
pliers, as shown in the illustration. Place one paper
clip on each battery terminal, holding the clips in
place with the rubber bands. Use the hot-melt glue
to secure the magnet. Pull the two ends of the coil

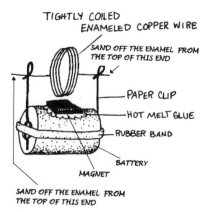

TIGHTLY COILED
ENAMELED COPPER WIRE

SAND OFF THE ENAMEL FROM
THE TOP OF THIS END

PAPER CLIP

HOT MELT GLUE

RUBBER BAND

BATTERY

MAGNET

SAND OFF THE ENAMEL FROM
THE TOP OF THIS END

out, opposite each other in a straight line, for about
3 inches (8 cm). Sand off about 1 inch (3 cm) of the

enamel coating from the top half of both ends of the coil. Place the coil in the paper clip supports. Start to spin the coil by hand. It will continue to spin until the battery wears down or you manually stop it.

A closeup of the coil and how the ends are sanded

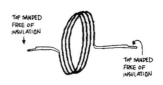

NOTE: This motor doesn't need a split ring commutator because it will continue to spin due to inertia when the enameled wire breaks the circuit. That inertial spin (see Book 2) will bring the bare copper wire in contact with the terminals to close the circuit once again after a half revolution.

Electric motors are used for many things in everyday life: tape players, VCRs, HO gauge electric trains, real electric trains, blenders, and pumps, to name a few. All of the motors work in pretty much the same way as the one described above.

ELECTRIC GENERATORS

In 1831 Faraday discovered that a magnet could produce an electric current when its lines of force cut across a copper wire. Electricity was generated *only* at the moment that the lines of force cut across the wire. The ebb and flow (coming and going) of the lines of force across the wire had to be continual to generate electricity for a prolonged time.

Faraday designed a wheel that would move through the magnet's lines of force as it rotated. As a new section of the wheel was constantly cutting across the lines of force, electricity was generated.

Basically, the generator is an electric motor in reverse. If you manually spin the motor, wire coils move around the magnet, and electricity is generated. In 1831 Joseph Henry developed the first practical electric motor. A generator works in just the opposite way from an electric motor. When a coil is turned in the presence of a magnetic field, electrical current is produced.

The necessary parts for a generator are a magnetic field, a coil of wire that rotates in the magnetic field, and a circuit to transmit the current outside the generator.

Experiment 15
APPARATUS

a small electric motor that can be powered by a C cell battery
a C cell battery
2 small pieces of wire
a small flashlight bulb
a variable-speed electric drill

PROCEDURE
Attach the C cell battery to the motor with the wire. The motor should start to spin. Remove the battery from the circuit and replace it with the bulb. Place the spindle (spinning part) of the motor in the jaws of the drill. Turn on the drill at slow speed. The bulb should light up.

A small electric motor

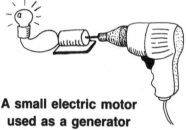

A small electric motor used as a generator

NOTE: The drill spins the motor rapidly enough to create an electric current that lights the bulb. This demonstration shows how a motor can also be used as a generator.

Remember:

♦ When a current is passed through a coil in the presence of a magnetic field, as in a motor, motion is the result.
♦ When a coil rotates in the presence of a magnetic field, as in a generator, electricity is the result.

A potential difference is produced when magnetic lines of force cut across a copper wire. As discussed in the Batteries section, when a potential difference exists in a closed circuit, an electric current is generated.

ALTERNATING CURRENT

Experiment 15 allows you to produce direct current, or current that moves in one direction. Direct current is produced because the type of motor/generator used had a split ring commutator (see page 93).

Many generators, however, produce *alternating current* (AC). Instead of using a split ring commutator, these generators use *slip rings*. The current produced first flows one way, then the other.

Alternating current is very useful in such applications as heating, lighting, and demagnetizing. It is much easier to send alternating current rather than direct current over large distances. Since the power sources that turn generators may be great distances from the area where the power is needed, alternating current is the preferred form of electrical power.

Alternating current can be sent over great distances because transformers can step it up to very high voltage. When the current (amperage) is low and the voltage high, very little energy is lost in the power transmission. The amperage is lowered and the voltage increased by putting the current through a transformer.

A transformer has no moving parts. The simplest step-up transformer is an iron core with a coil of few windings on one side and a coil of many windings on the other.

EDDY CURRENTS

Induced currents from the metal parts of machinery or circuitry are called *eddy currents*. These currents sometimes arise by accident and can cause problems in the operation of a circuit. However, they can also be put to good use.

For example, eddy currents are used in industry to heat metal parts without the direct application of heat. The metal is placed in an alternating current field. The eddy currents created by the field cause the metal to get hot.

When a conductor is passed close to a magnetic field, the eddy currents produced set up an electrical field in the conductor. These induced eddy currents can retard the movement of a magnet.

The application of these eddy currents can be seen in household electric meters and automobile speedometers.

Trick 11
The Confusing Pendulum
EFFECT: You hand a spectator two identical pendulums to hold. You start them swinging in exactly the

same way. In a moment, you say the magic word, and one of the pendulums slows down while the other one keeps on swinging.

PROPS
    2 pieces of string
    a bar magnet
    a copper bar identical in size to the bar magnet
    a copper sheet
    a small can of spray paint

SETUP
Spray paint the magnet and the copper bar so they look the same. Place a mark on the magnet so you will be able to identify it.
    Tie one string around the center of the magnet. Tie the other string around the bar. The length of both strings should be identical.
    Place the copper sheet on the tabletop.

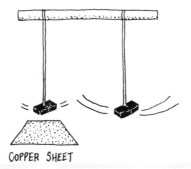

COPPER SHEET

METHOD
Make sure that both of the pendulums are swinging over the copper sheet. The eddy current set up over the copper sheet will slow down the magnet.

If your audience is unaware of eddy currents, they will not have a clue to how this works. Even if they think a magnet may be involved, when they place the magnetic pendulum over the copper sheet, there will be no attraction. The only magnetic activity occurs when the magnet is moving past the copper sheet.

When I was experimenting with this, I timed the two pendulums. I started the pendulums swinging with arcs of identical length. Then the plain pendulum continued swinging for a little over sixty seconds. The magnetic pendulum stopped swinging in about thirty seconds.

SUPPLIERS

When asking for any of these catalogs, please mention that you saw the company's name in one of Bob Friedhoffer's books.

Johnson Smith Co.
P.O. Box 25500
Bradenton, Florida 34206-5500

Free catalog from one of the original novelty supply companies in the country

Edmund Scientific
101 E. Gloucester Pike
Barrington, New Jersey 08007-1380

Free catalog full of good things for the budding scientist

Morris & Lee Inc.
85 Botsford Place
Buffalo, New York 14216

Send for free catalog of genuine scientific apparatus at great prices

AIN Plastics
300 Park Avenue South
New York, New York 10010

Source for plastic "crystal balls" and fiberoptic rods; drop them a note to ask them about cost and availability

Mickey Hades International
Box 1414
Calgary, Alberta
Canada T2P 2L6

Send for free price list of great selection of magic books from the largest magical publisher

Paul Diamond's Mail Order Magic
P.O. Box 11570
Fort Lauderdale, Florida 33339

Good prices, good tricks, price list—$1.50; mail order only

Zanadu
772 Newark Avenue
Jersey City, New Jersey 07306

$.50 for catalog of exclusive magic effects; mail order only

Louis Tannen Inc.
6 West 32nd St.
New York, New York 10001-3808

Ask to be placed on the free mailing list of one of America's largest magic stores; visit when you're in New York

Hank Lee's Magic Factory
125 Lincoln St.
Boston, Massachusetts 02205

Ask to be placed on the free mailing list of one of America's finest and largest magic stores; visit when you're in Boston

Abbot's Magic Co.
Colon, Michigan 49040

Ask the cost of the huge catalog filled with goodies

Land of Magic
450 N.E. 20th Street
Boca Raton, Florida 33431

A great retail magic and novelty store; free mail order catalog for the asking

FOR. FURTHER READING

Asimov, Isaac. *Asimov's Chronology of Science and Discovery.* New York: Harper & Row, 1989.

Bobo, J. B. *Coin Magic.* New York: Dover Publications, 1982.

Epstein, Lewis Carroll. *Thinking Physics.* San Francisco: Insight Press, 1979–1988.

Gardner, Martin. *Encyclopedia of Impromptu Magic.* Chicago: Magic Inc., 1978.

Gardner, Robert. *Famous Experiments You Can Do.* New York: Franklin Watts, 1990.

Gonick, Larry. *The Cartoon Guide to Physics.* New York: Harper Perennial, 1991.

Macauly, David. *The Way Things Work.* Boston: Houghton-Mifflin, 1988.

Tarbell, Harlan. *Tarbell Course in Magic, Vols. 1–7.* New York: Louis Tannen.

Walker, Jearl. *The Flying Circus of Physics.* New York: Wiley and Sons, 1977.

INDEX

ABOUT THE AUTHOR

Bob Friedhoffer has been an active, professional magician for over twenty years, performing all over the world in various places such as universities, comedy clubs, night clubs, libraries, museums, and truly prestigious venues such as the White House in Washington, D.C. His extensive traveling as a performer and author still takes him all over the world, though currently he is devoting much of his time to performing his live science/magic show at many schools and museums in the United States.

Though his University of Miami degree is a BBA in accounting, Mr. Friedhoffer's studies as an undergraduate involved numerous science courses. He is currently finishing up a Master's program entitled Science and Society at the City University of New York.